GW00497194

Road

A prayer guide for Eastertide

- with Novena for Pentecost -

All booklets are published thanks to the generous support of the members of the Catholic Truth Society

A GOODNEWS PUBLICATION

CATHOLIC TRUTH SOCIETY
PUBLISHERS TO THE HOLY SEE

Contents

Be Open to Pentecost

As Christians, we celebrate Christmas and Easter, but Pentecost – the third element of the Good News of Salvation – seems to be rather neglected. This prayer guide is to help Christians to be open to a personal Pentecost in their own lives, and to pray for a new Pentecost on the earth, so that the life changing power of the Gospel can be proclaimed and experienced.

God has already sent Jesus as Saviour of the world. Through his birth, death, and resurrection, Jesus restored the human race to right order with God. But do we see the kingdom of God in our world today, amid wars, breakdown of the family and of the environment, economic crises, social injustice, and divisions amongst Christians?

Before he ascended into heaven, Jesus told his disciples to wait for "the promise of the Father about which you have heard me speak; for John baptized with water, but in a few days you will be baptized with the Holy Spirit... [and] you will receive power when the Holy Spirit comes upon you" (*Ac* 1:4,5,8). It is this power of the Holy Spirit that puts into effect the saving action of Jesus, who has been sent to complete the work of salvation on earth and to bring us the fullness of grace.

A time and place

Often we don't have time to get away so this prayer guide is to help you have a retreat at home and to prepare for Pentecost. A retreat is a time you set aside for God so that he can speak to you. Choose a specific place and time for prayer (it need only be ten minutes) and keep to that time every day if possible.

Contemplating the history of salvation

Just as Jesus explained God's plan of salvation to the disciples on the Road to Emmaus, so you are invited to meditate on this story over a period of 40 days. Jesus wants to reveal to you who he is, what he has done, what God's plan is for mankind and where you fit into it. This has been revealed through the Scriptures and through the Church.

The forty days journey

- We begin this journey on Easter Sunday.
- Each of these days is set out in the booklet, over six weeks (*See p.8*).
- Before you begin your daily meeting with Jesus you might want to ask the Holy Spirit to help you, using your own words, or words given us by the Church, such as: "Come Holy Spirit, fill the hearts of your faithful, and kindle in us the fire of your love!"

- Every day offers a verse from the Bible, a short meditation, a brief explanation from the Catechism of the Catholic Church, and a prayer.
- Don't just read the text, but think about it and maybe memorize the line of Scripture and recall it during the day.
- You also may want to read the day's theme again before you go to bed.
- There are also some useful prayers to the Holy Spirit at the end of the booklet which you might like to use.

The nine days to Pentecost

After the 40 days you are then invited to pray a Novena (nine days of prayer) which ends on the vigil of Pentecost (*See p.58*).

- Each day of the Novena is set out in the booklet.
- There is a special intercession for each day.
- Each day offers a passage of Scripture, a reflection, and a prayer.
- There are also additional prayers you can chose from if you wish.

Celebrate Pentecost

We hope as a result you may be inspired to organize some special event in your parish or prayer group on Pentecost Sunday or meet with other Christians.

Beginning with Moses and all the prophets, he interpreted to them what referred to him in all the scriptures (Lk 24:27).

We are told in the Gospel of Mark that Jesus never taught without using parables, but later, "when he was alone with his disciples, he explained everything to them" (*Mk* 4:34). Likewise with 'his' story of Salvation. After Jesus was raised from the dead He walked with his bewildered, frightened disciples. Despite having been with him for three years they did not recognize him. During these forty days Jesus had to prepare his disciples to receive the Holy Spirit who would bring to perfection in them all that the Father had promised since the beginning of time: a church, a people, a bride for his Son.

Recognizing Jesus in the Old Testament through the writings of Moses and all the prophets is the journey Jesus wants to take you and me on now. We are in a season of great shaking and unbelief in the world, and you and I and all the members of God's people filled with his Holy Spirit can rejoice through all these difficulties because we have this glorious hope to which we have been called (cf *Ep* 1:18).

After we each make this journey alone with Jesus we will come to the last nine days before Pentecost, when we will begin to pray together for a new Pentecost as the disciples did in the Upper Room.

Prayer

Jesus, as I make this journey with you from your Resurrection to Pentecost, I pray that you would open my eyes and my heart to the Father's plan of salvation, and prepare my heart for a new Pentecost along with all the Body of Christ.

∽ THE CREATION AND FALL ∽
FIRST WEEK

Day 1: Known and loved

Even before he made the world, God loved us and chose us in Christ. (Ep 1:4)

The book of Genesis starts, "In the beginning..." and this would be a good place to start our journey. But before we do that let's look at what St Paul says in Ephesians above. Here is that wonderful mystery that even before the world was created you were already known, loved, and chosen in Christ.

When a potter starts to make a pot he already sees the finished product in his mind. However for that pot to be made the clay has to be pliable. We have to be willing to be moved by the Potter's hands into his vision for us.

PRAYER: *Father, thank you for your love for me and for the vision you have of me as your perfect work of art. Help me to say 'yes' to you.*

CATECHISM: For if man exists, it is because God has created him through love, and through love continues to hold him in existence. (*CCC*, 1)

SCRIPTURE: *Ps* 139:16; *Ep* 2:10

Day 2: God's desire for union

Let us create man in our own image to be like us. (Gn 1:26)

Who is this Creator God? He speaks of himself in Genesis as being "us". It is easier to see this when we read Jn 14:9 ('I am in the Father and the Father is in Me.') and *Gn* 1:2: ('the Spirit of God hovered over the surface of the water.') He is Three-in-One and there is perfect fellowship in that communion of Persons. The Spirit of God is the Love that continually flows between the Father and the Son. When God created Adam and Eve he invited them into this fellowship. Your Father is now reaching out his hand to you.

PRAYER: *Father, you have revealed yourself to us through Jesus your Son and have now given us your Holy Spirit. Thank you for your invitation to live and move in you.*

CATECHISM: God himself is an eternal exchange of love, Father, Son and Holy Spirit, and he has destined us to share in that exchange. (*CCC, 221*)

SCRIPTURE: *Jn* 17:26

Day 3: You bring joy to God's heart

Then God looked over all he had made and he saw that it was very good. (*Gn* 1:31)

Have you sat back and enjoyed your own work of art? A newly decorated house, a meal, a poem, a painting? Isn't it a wonderful feeling! Your Creator-Father-God's heart bursts with joy when he looks at you.

Ah but you say, 'I am not good! I don't deserve his love.' That's true, but "now there is no condemnation for those who belong to Christ Jesus" (*Rm* 8:1). Trust this word today. You belong to him and he delights in you!

PRAYER: *You made me, you created me. Now give me the sense to follow your commands. May all who fear you find in me a cause for joy for I have put my hope in your word.* (cf *Ps* 119:73,74)

CATECHISM: God's love for Israel is compared to a father's love for his son. His love for his people is stronger than a mother's for her children. God loves his people more than a bridegroom his beloved... (*CCC*, 219)

SCRIPTURE: *Rm* 5:1; *Jr* 31:3

Day 4: Where are you?

When Adam sinned, sin entered the world. (*Rm* 5:12)

There was one thing God asked Adam not to do: "But the Lord God warned him: you may freely eat the fruit of every tree in the garden – except the fruit of the tree of the knowledge of good and evil. If you eat its fruit you are sure to die "(*Gn* 2:16-17).

Right at the beginning of his story, man falls. Tempted by the evil, one man abuses his freedom and loses his likeness with God. Man's downfall is that he wants to makes himself God!

"At that moment their eyes were opened and they suddenly felt shame at their nakedness. And when they heard God walking in the garden they were afraid and hid because they were naked" (*Gn* 3:7,8).

PRAYER: *Lord of heaven and earth, forgive me for the times when I chose to do wrong and hid because of my sin. Nothing is hidden from you. Cause me to bend my knee to you, my Lord and King.*

CATECHISM: The account of the fall in Genesis 3 uses figurative language, but affirms a primeval event, a deed that took place at the beginning of the history of man. (*CCC*, 390)

SCRIPTURE: *Heb* 4:13

Day 5: Battling to be good!

For the sin of this one man, Adam, caused death to rule over many. (Rm 5:17)

God's creation has received a severe wound. We who were made in the image and likeness of God remain in his image but lose our 'likeness' which is God's Spirit.

This wound of sin has placed Satan as 'prince of this world', so for me to be Christian I must go against the flow. We have no power to do this on our own.

How many times have you decided to do good and found yourself doing the opposite? Take a little time to think honestly about your own inability to be good, your weakness, your wounds, your sins.

PRAYER: *Father, because of the fall I was born with a wound. I come to you today with all my heavy baggage of sin, selfishness and pain. Only you can fight my battles. Only you can carry me through the storms of life.*

CATECHISM: As a result of original sin, human nature is weakened in its powers; subject to ignorance, suffering, and the domination of death; and inclined to sin. (This inclination is called 'concupiscence.') (*CCC*, 418)

SCRIPTURE: *Rm 7:15-19*

Day 6: Return and rest

So the Lord God banished them from the garden.
(Gn 3:23)

God is all good and cannot dwell with sin, but in his great love he does not leave us abandoned to our selfish lives. Look at these beautiful words of God: "Does a woman forget her baby, or a mother the child within her womb? Yet, even if these forget, I will never forget my own" (*Is* 49:15).

The desire of the Father's heart is that we return to him. As St Augustine said: "Our hearts are restless until they rest in you."

PRAYER: *Lord I thank you that you never abandon those you love. You do not leave me to the consequence of my sin. Thank you for your heart of love. Cause me to worship you and love you with all my heart.*

CATECHISM: The desire for God is written in the human heart, because man is created by God and for God; and God never ceases to draw man to himself. Only in God will he find the truth and the happiness he never stops searching for. (*CCC*, 1)

SCRIPTURE: *Ps* 62:1-2

Day 7: Our weakness – an opportunity for God's power

When I am weak then I am strong. (2 *Co* 12:10)

Yes, Adam messed it up! Did God know that he would? Yes he did! Then why did God let him?

For us to be fully made in God's image and likeness in more than just name, we had to have the power of free will. God wants us to want him to be God. As we move on through this "story of Salvation" we will see that God introduces himself to the people of Israel as a covenant-keeping God. God will always keep his side of the Covenant, but will man keep his? We know the answer to this, over and over we depend on ourselves and fall flat on our faces, instead of relying on and being obedient to God.

PRAYER: *Lord as you introduced yourself to Abraham, Isaac and Jacob as a God who makes promises and who walks closely to his people, teach me what it means to bow my knee in my weakness in order to see your Lordship and power in my life.*

CATECHISM: God created man a rational being, conferring on him the dignity of a person who can initiate and control his own actions. 'God willed that man should be "left in the hand of his own counsel", so that he might of his own accord seek his Creator and freely attain his full and blessed perfection by cleaving to him.'(*CCC*, 1730 i)

SCRIPTURE: *Ph* 4:13

⟋⟍ GOD CALLS A PEOPLE TO BE HIS OWN ⟋⟍
SECOND WEEK

Day 1: Abraham our father in faith

Abraham was, humanly speaking, the founder of our Jewish nation. (Rm 4:1)

The whole of the Old Testament recounts the relationship between the Jewish nation and their God. He chose them for his own purposes (cf *Rm* 9:11) to reveal himself and his whole plan of Salvation to mankind. In Genesis 12, verse 1, we read that God called Abraham to leave his native country (symbolizing the world), for a land which he would show him. Abraham obeyed and Hebrews 11:8 says: "He went out not knowing where he was going."

When we read about Abraham's call it is very reminiscent of the call of the first disciples to leave all and follow Jesus. "Faith is the confidence that what we hope for will actually happen; it gives us assurance about the things we cannot see" (*Heb* 11:1). Faith is a gift.

When you and I respond to God's call we take the same steps of faith. It's like any relationship: at first we may not know where we are going, but with time we learn to trust his voice and his leading.

PRAYER: *Father, reveal to me your character as you revealed it to your chosen people. Give me your gift of faith to hear your voice and to respond to your call.*

CATECHISM: Faith is a gift of God, a supernatural virtue infused by him. "Before this faith can be exercised, man must have the grace of God to move and assist him; he must have the interior help of the Holy Spirit, who moves the heart and converts it to God, who opens the eyes of the mind and 'makes it easy for all to accept and believe the truth.'" (*CCC*, 153)

SCRIPTURE: *Ga* 3:6-9

Day 2: Believe God's promises to you

I will make you into a great nation. (*Gn* 12:2)

It's all very well believing something that is possible, but what if everything is shouting to you: "It's out of the question! Absolutely impossible!" We do well to trust God and not work things out on our own. Abraham and Sarah, being so old, could not see how God's promises could be fulfilled in them so they made their own plans (cf. *Gn*, chapter 16). Sarah asked Abraham to "sleep with my servant Hagar "("Perhaps I can have children through her") and Hagar gave birth to Ishmael (child of the Law). However, in Chapter 21 we read that the Lord kept his word and did for Sarah exactly what He had promised... she gave birth to Isaac (child of the promise). This happened at just the time God said it would.

PRAYER: *Father, I see many situations in my life that are impossible for me to change. Give me the faith to trust that you can do the impossible and bring glory to your Name.*

CATECHISM: Believing is possible only by grace and the interior help of the Holy Spirit. But it is no less true that believing is an authentically human act.

In faith, the human intellect and will cooperate with divine grace. (*CCC*, 154,155)

SCRIPTURE: *Pr* 3:5-6

Day 3: The Father and the Son

Abraham, who had received God's promises, was ready to sacrifice his only son, Isaac. (Heb 11:17)

In chapter 22 of Genesis we learn so much about the character of God as Father and Son. Abraham was willing to sacrifice his only son, the son who would become a great nation. And Isaac carried the wood for the burnt offering and was willingly tied to the altar. Isaac trusted his Father, and Abraham his God. As his hand was raised to slay his son God said, "Do not hurt him, for now I know you really fear God" (*Gn* 22:12).

PRAYER: *Father, when I think too much is being asked of me, help me to trust that you will provide the offering.*

CATECHISM: What moves us to believe is not the fact that revealed truths appear as true and intelligible in the light of our natural reason: we believe "because of the authority of God himself who reveals them, who can neither deceive nor be deceived." Faith is certain. It is more certain than all human knowledge because it is founded on the very word of God who cannot lie. (*CCC*, 156,157)

SCRIPTURE: *Heb* 11:17-19

Day 4: Changed by his call and his blessing

The God of our Fathers, Abraham, Isaac, and Jacob...
(*Ex* 3:15)

All the way through the Old Testament the Israelites refer
to the three Patriarchal figures - Abraham, Isaac and Jacob
– and yet, when we read their stories we can't help but see
their humanity. God was teaching his people about the
power of his blessing when He calls us by name.

Jacob, Isaac's son, the twin of Esau, stole his brother's
birthright and blessing, but on his way to making peace
with his brother we read that he wrestles with God for a
blessing (cf. *Gn* 32:22). That night, God says to Jacob,
"From now on you will be called Israel because you have
fought with God and won." Jacob returns to Bethel,
where he builds an altar "to the God who answered my
prayers when I was in distress. He has been with me
wherever I have gone" (*Gn* 35:3).

PRAYER: *When you call us, Lord, you change our name.
We may be called "wounded, outcast, lonely, afraid" but
you call us "confidence, joyfulness, overcoming-one,
faithfulness, friend of God, one who seeks my face." Help
me to receive your blessing today.*

CATECHISM: The human heart is heavy and hardened. God must give man a new heart. Conversion is first of all a work of the grace of God, who makes our hearts return to him: "Restore us to thyself, O Lord, that we may be restored!" God gives us the strength to begin anew. (*CCC*, 1432)

SCRIPTURE: *Ac* 3:13

Day 5: Gifted by God

For I myself shall give you a wisdom in speaking that all your adversaries will be powerless to resist or refute. (Lk 21:15)

More than ten chapters of Genesis take us through the story of Joseph. The favourite son of his father is sold by his brothers and becomes a slave in Egypt. God's hand of blessing and covenant love makes him outstandingly gifted. Through the interpretation of Pharaoh's dreams he is released from prison and given responsibility in Pharaoh's palace. His wisdom and integrity win him favour, and ultimately, his love and forgiveness of his brothers who had considered him dead saved them and gave them new life.

PRAYER: *Jesus, over and over in the Scriptures you reveal your commitment of love for your people. Give me the grace today to love you and my brothers and sisters around me.*

CATECHISM: God's Spirit prepares for the time of the Messiah. Neither is fully revealed but both are already promised, to be watched for and welcomed at the time of their manifestation. So, for this reason, when the Church reads the Old Testament, she searches there for what the Spirit, "who has spoken to us through the prophets," wants to tell us about Christ. (*CCC*, 702)

SCRIPTURE: *Jr* 1:5-9

Day 6: The darkness cannot put out the light

I came into the world as light, so that everyone who believes in me might not remain in darkness. (*Jn* 12:46)

Time and time again the people of Israel and beyond were called to remain faithful under the oppression of darkness and unbelief. When Joseph died "a new king came to power in Egypt who knew nothing about Joseph or what he had done" (*Ex* 1:8). This new king was afraid that the Israelites would over-run their land. Terrible restrictions were put on them, and we read in Exodus 1:22 that all first-born Hebrew boys were thrown into the Nile.

As Christians, we are called today to let the light of Christ shine always in our hearts. When the leaders of our land are not Christian we are called to remain faithful to the teaching of Jesus.

PRAYER: *Jesus, so few know you today and your people are persecuted in many countries. Equip your people with a steadfast faith and unity to be a light in the darkness.*

CATECHISM: In Jesus Christ, the whole of God's truth has been made manifest. "Full of grace and truth," he came as the "light of the world," he is the Truth. "Whoever believes in me may not remain in darkness." (*CCC*, 2466)

SCRIPTURE: 1 *P* 2:9

Day 7: God's almighty hand!

Then Israel arrived in Egypt... the Lord multiplied the people of Israel until they became too mighty for their enemies. Then he turned the Egyptians against the Israelites. (Ps 105:23-25)

Could this possibly be a misprint in the word of God - that God turned the hearts of the Egyptians against his own people. Our Father allows difficult situations, misunderstandings, oppressions, to come to those he loves for the very purpose of drawing us closer to him and showing us that he is our safe refuge. He is a tower of strength in time of need.

PRAYER: *Lord, help me to trust that you will save me in my time of trouble. Increase my faith and comfort me in my own personal situation. Help me to encourage and comfort others in their difficulties.*

CATECHISM: In time we can discover that God in his almighty providence can bring a good from the consequences of an evil, even a moral evil, caused by his creatures... From the greatest moral evil ever committed – the rejection and murder of God's only Son, caused by the sins of all men – God, by his grace that "abounded all the more," brought the greatest of goods: the glorification of Christ and our redemption. (*CCC*, 312)

SCRIPTURE: *Jm* 1:2-4; *Rm* 5:3-5; 1 *P* 1:6-7

∼ GOD RESCUES HIS PEOPLE ∼
AND GIVES THEM THE LAW
THIRD WEEK

Day 1: Just in time

God heard their groaning, and he remembered his covenant promise to Abraham, Isaac and Jacob. He looked down on the people of Israel and knew it was time to act. (Ex 3:24-25)

God promised to rescue his people from the oppression of the Egyptians and lead them to freedom. God was waiting for his time to act; he heard the cry of his people and began his plan of deliverance from the power of sin (Egypt) and the works of the flesh (fallen humanity). "When we were utterly helpless, Christ came at just the right time and died for us sinners." (*Rm* 5:6)

PRAYER: *When I am faced with my own sinfulness, help me not to feel trapped and enslaved by it. Lord come to save me in my utter helplessness.*

CATECHISM: The Scriptures had foretold this divine plan of salvation through the putting to death of 'the righteous one, my Servant' as a mystery of universal redemption, that is, as the ransom that would free men from the slavery of sin. (*CCC*, 601)

SCRIPTURE: *Jr* 2:20

Day 2: No forgiveness without bloodshed

He is so rich in kindness and grace that he purchased our freedom with the blood of his Son and forgave our sins. (Ep 1:7)

The first Passover is the climax of the deliverance of God's people out of Egypt. "The blood on your door posts will serve as a sign, marking the houses where you are staying. When I see the blood of the lamb, I will pass over you" (*Ex* 12:13). As the blood of the lamb saved the Israelites from the plague of death, Jesus' blood given for you and me on the Cross washes us from our sin (cf 1 *Jn* 1:7) and reconciles us with God. At the last supper, on the day of the Passover, Jesus says, " This is my blood, which confirms the covenant between God and his people. It is poured out as a sacrifice for many" (*Mk* 14:24). Moses was called to believe in the power of his God, and we too are called to believe in the saving blood of Jesus.

PRAYER: *Jesus, I believe you died for me and shed your blood for me. Today I kneel at the foot of your cross. Cleanse me from my sin, and make me whiter than snow.*

CATECHISM: On account of sin, God 'made him to be sin who knew no sin, so that we might become the righteousness of God.' (*CCC*, 602)

SCRIPTURE: *Ac* 20:28

Day 3: Fear robs faith

The Lord himself will fight for you. Just stay calm.
(*Ex* 14:14)

Pharaoh is not so easily defeated and continues to follow the Israelites as they go into the wilderness as far as the Red Sea. The fear of being trapped attacks their faith in Moses and their God. They complain and wish to be slaves in Egypt again.

When all seems to be going well, it is so easy to hold on to faith. How often does fear rob you of your faith? Moses tells the people "Don't be afraid. Just stand still and watch the Lord rescue you today" (*Ex* 14:13).

I am reminded of the time Jesus was asleep in the boat with his disciples and a storm arises. Jesus wakes and rebukes the wind and the raging waves. He says to his disciples, " Where is your faith?" (*Lk* 8:24).

PRAYER: *Lord strengthen my faith, so that when I face difficulties, fear will not rob me. Help me to stand still and know that you are my God.*

CATECHISM: To obey (from the Latin *ob-audire*, to 'hear or listen to') in faith is to submit freely to the word that has been heard, because its truth is guaranteed by God, who is Truth itself. (*CCC*, 144)

SCRIPTURE: *Ps* 46:10

Day 4: You are God's very own

"You know how I carried you on eagle's wings and brought you to myself." (*Ex* 19 v. 4)

The Israelites, as we all know, did not go immediately into the Promised Land. The wilderness was the place of learning to 'let God be God'! The journey should have taken them only a few years by foot, but it took them forty years! God was longing for them to be a people of worship and trust, but at every difficulty - thirst, hunger, fear, and battle - they would not learn and went round and round in circles.

Every new moment in our lives is given to us to love, worship and trust our Lord. Yes, he carries you "on eagle's wings".

PRAYER: *Lord, cause my soul to rest in you today. Teach me to worship you at every moment and allow you to be Lord of my life. Carry me on your eagle's wings.*

CATECHISM: 'We know that in everything God works for good for those who love him.' The constant witness of the saints confirms this truth: St Catherine of Siena said to 'those who are scandalized and rebel against what happens to them': 'Everything comes from love, all is ordained for the salvation of man, God does nothing without this goal in mind.' (*CCC*, 313)

SCRIPTURE: *Is* 40:31

Day 5: After fifty days

*Now if you will obey me and keep my covenant, you will
be my own special treasure from among all the peoples
on earth; for all the earth belongs to me. And you will be
my kingdom of priests, my holy nation. (Ex 10:5-6)*

God calls Moses to climb mount Sinai where he is given
the Ten Commandments and the Law. God's people were
being taught the ways of their God, a way of life so very
different from the one lived by mankind at that time. God
promised to be their God, if they obeyed him.

   Does this sound familiar to you? Even Adam could not
obey! God's Covenant was impossible to keep! That's
because its job is to highlight our sinfulness and show
that we are unable to keep God's commandments by our
own efforts.

PRAYER: *Lord I thank you that you did not leave me in a
hopeless situation of continual defeat. Thank you for the
promise of a second covenant, where my true liberty is
found in absolute dependence on you.*

CATECHISM: According to Christian tradition, the Law is
holy, spiritual and good, yet still imperfect. Like a tutor it
shows what must be done, but does not of itself give the
strength, the grace of the Spirit, to fulfill it. (*CCC*, 1963)

SCRIPTURE: *Ti* 2:13-14

Day 6: Another fifty days

But this is the new covenant I will make with the people of Israel on that day, says the Lord. I will put my instructions deep within them, and I will write them on their hearts. I will be their God, and they will be my people. (Jr 31:33)

Remember when God promised Abraham a son? He and Sarah, through their own efforts, first had Ishmael born of a slave, and then Isaac was born of God's promise. One was cast out and the other was to be heir of all. This foreshadowed the old and new covenant.

The giving of the Law fifty days after the Passover also foreshadows Pentecost: the giving of the Holy Spirit fifty days after the Resurrection. At the giving of the Law three thousand people died (cf. *Ex* 23:38); at Pentecost three thousand were saved! The Law, we are told in Galatians 3:24, "was our guardian until Christ came; it protected us until we could be made right with God through faith."

The fact that you believe that Jesus loves you, and that he died and rose for you, means that you have been made righteous in him through faith, and not by the keeping of the Law. Receiving the Holy Spirit gives us the grace to live a life pleasing to God. Through the power of the Holy Spirit God writes his law on our hearts!

PRAYER: *Lord I thank you for this wonderful news. Thank you for being my righteousness. Give me an open heart to your Holy Spirit. Come and write your law on my heart so that I will be pleasing to you.*

CATECHISM: The New Law is called a law of love because it makes us act out of love infused by the Holy Spirit, rather than from fear; a law of grace because it confers the strength of grace to act, by means of faith and the sacraments. (*CCC*, 1972)

SCRIPTURE: *Jr* 31:34

Day 7: A wonderful place of rest

God's promise of entering his rest still stands, so we ought to tremble with fear that some of you might fail to experience it. (Heb 4:1)

The Israelites were led out of Egypt through the wilderness in order to dwell in the Promised Land. This land was to be a place of rest. They would still have battles but they would know victory through their trust in God.

We have a very important lesson to learn from the Israelites: they did not go in to take possession of the land because of fear of the 'giants' in the land! They took no notice of God's promise: "Don't be shocked or afraid of them! The Lord your God is going ahead of you. He will fight for you, just as you saw him do in Egypt" (*Dt* 1:29-30). They disobeyed God! Because of this Moses is remembered as the 'man of the Law' and was refused entrance to the Promised Land. Joshua, however, known as the 'man of Grace' (another forerunner of Jesus), continued to lead the people to take possession of the land. This is our calling: to enter God's rest. Jesus is our rest!

PRAYER: *Jesus, you remind us that we have all we need to fight the battles that we face each day. Lead me today into your rest, a rest from my labours, and real trust that you come alongside me and fight with me.*

CATECHISM: With creation, God does not abandon his creatures to themselves. He not only gives them being and existence, but also, and at every moment, upholds and sustains them in being, enables them to act and brings them to their final end. (*CCC*, 301)

SCRIPTURE: *Mt* 11:28-29

~ PREDICTIONS OF THE MESSIAH ~
SIGNS OF GOD'S KINGDOM
FOURTH WEEK

Day 1: God reveals his secrets
to those he loves

Indeed the Sovereign Lord never does anything until he reveals his plans to his servants the prophets. (Am 3:7)

Not only did God choose to speak to us through the lives of his people, he gave the power of the Holy Spirit to prophets to speak of the Messiah who was to come in the future. In fact, there are two predictions of the coming of a Messiah: that he would come as a man suffering and as a King . It was part of God's plan that the Jews did not recognize their Messiah in Jesus, so that there would be a time for the Gentiles (the Church) to be saved. Now we should pray that they, and all mankind, would know and recognize Jesus as their Saviour, so that when he comes as King in Glory 'every knee shall bow and every tongue confess that Jesus Christ is Lord'.

PRAYER: *Father open my eyes to see you in the scriptures. Send your Holy Spirit on me and all your people to reveal to us your secret plans.*

CATECHISM: God inspired the human authors of the sacred books. 'To compose the sacred books, God chose certain men who, all the while he employed them in this task, made full use of their own faculties and powers so that, though he acted in them and by them, it was as true authors that they consigned to writing whatever he wanted, and no more'. (*CCC*, 106)

SCRIPTURE: *Mk* 4:11

Day 2: A man after God's own heart

Your rod and your staff they comfort me. (*Ps* 23:4)

David was humble and dependent on God, and the Holy Spirit inspired his writings. Today we shall look at Psalm 22. Jesus himself quotes this Psalm in his last words on the cross. He recognized himself in David's words: "My God, my God, why have you abandoned me?"

> "But I am a worm and a not a man.
> I am scorned and despised by all!
> Everyone who sees me mocks me.
> They sneer and shake their heads, saying,
> 'Is this the one who relies on the Lord?
> Then let the Lord save him!
> If the Lord loves him so much,
> Let the Lord rescue him!'"

PRAYER: *Lord, help me through the power of your Holy Spirit to read and know the Scriptures so that I too may find comfort in them as you did on the cross.*

CATECHISM: The Holy Spirit gives a spiritual understanding of the Word of God to those who read or hear it, according to the dispositions of their hearts. (*CCC*, 1101)

SCRIPTURE: *Ps* 119:72

Day 3: The wisdom of Solomon

Beautiful words stir my heart. I will recite a lovely poem about the king, for my tongue is like the pen of a skilled poet. (Ps 45)

Solomon, we are told, "composed some 3000 proverbs and 1005 songs" (cf. 1 *K* 4:32). In Psalm 72:12-14, he writes:

> "He will rescue the poor when they cry to him;
> he will help the oppressed,
> who have no one to defend them.
> He feels pity for the weak and the needy,
> and he will rescue them."

What a wonderful glimpse of the Kingdom of God.

PRAYER: *Our Father in Heaven, may your name be kept holy. May your Kingdom come soon. May your will be done on earth, as it is in heaven. Give us today the food we need, and forgive us our sins, as we have forgiven those who sin against us. And do not let us yield to temptation, but rescue us from the evil one* (cf. *Mt* 6:10-13).

CATECHISM: Prayed by Christ and fulfilled in Him, the Psalms remain essential to the prayer of the Church. (*CCC*, 2586)

SCRIPTURE: 2 *P* 1:20-21

Day 4: A King of peace

*"Out of the stump of David's family will grow a shoot –
yes a new branch bearing fruit from the old root. (Is 11:1)*

Jesus said, "Behold I am making all things new" (*Rv* 21:5),
and Isaiah speaks of Jesus as the 'new branch': And the
Spirit of the Lord will rest on him. The Spirit of wisdom
and understanding, the Spirit of counsel and might, the
Spirit of knowledge and fear of the Lord. (*Is* 11:2)

The Spirit of God rests on Jesus. All the fruits and gifts
of the Holy Spirit are found in him. Especially the gift of
Peace. When he appeared to his disciples after his
Resurrection he said, " My peace I give you" (*Jn* 20:19).

PRAYER: *Jesus, through your death and resurrection you
made all things new. You released on your people the gift
of your Spirit to build a church who would live your
kingdom here on earth. "Come Holy Spirit, fill the hearts
of your faithful and enkindle in them the fire of your love."*

CATECHISM: 'The kingdom of God [is] righteousness
and peace and joy in the Holy Spirit.' The end-time in
which we live is the age of the outpouring of the Spirit.
(*CCC*, 2819)

SCRIPTURE: *Jn* 14:27

Day 5: The suffering servant

My servant grew up in the Lord's presence like a tender green shoot, like a root in dry ground. (Is 53:2)

Jesus, "though he was God, he did not think of equality with God as something to cling to. Instead he gave up his divine privileges, he took the humble position as a slave" (*Ph* 2:6). The whole of Isaiah 53 prophesies of the death of Jesus on the cross. It clearly was no mistake!

"But it was the Lord's good plan to crush him and cause him grief."(v. 10)

"Because of his experience, my righteous servant will make it possible for many to be counted righteous, for he will bear all their sins... " (v. 11)

"Because he exposed himself to death, he was counted among the sinners. He bore the sins of many and interceded for sinners." (v. 12)

Jesus is now seated at the right hand of the Father continually interceding for us.

PRAYER: *Jesus you faced all the same testings we do, yet you did not sin. Because of you I can enter boldly into your throne room, to receive your mercy and to find grace to help in time of need (cf. Heb 4:16).*

CATECHISM: No man, not even the holiest, was ever able to take on himself the sins of all men and offer himself as a sacrifice for all. The existence in Christ of the divine person of the Son, who at once surpasses and embraces all human persons, and constitutes himself as the Head of all mankind, makes possible his redemptive sacrifice for all. (*CCC*, 616)

SCRIPTURE: *Heb* 4:16

Day 6: Signs of the Kingdom of God

He has sent me to comfort the broken-hearted and to proclaim that captives will be released and prisoners will be freed. (*Is* 61:1b)

John the Baptist told his disciples to ask Jesus, "Are you the Messiah we've been expecting, or should we keep looking for someone else?" Jesus sends his message: "... tell him what you have seen and heard: the blind see, the lame walk, the lepers are cured, the deaf hear, the dead are raised to life, and the Good News is being preached to the poor" (*Lk* 7:18-22). After Jesus reads Isaiah 61 in the synagogue he says, "The Scripture you've just heard has been fulfilled this very day!" (*Lk* 4:18) On another occasion he exclaimed, "I must preach the Good News of the Kingdom of God in other towns, too, because that is why I was sent" (*Lk* 4:43).

PRAYER: *Father, Jesus was sent by you. In the same way Jesus has commissioned and sent out his apostles ('sent ones'). I pray for all those following the call today to proclaim your Good News.*

CATECHISM: The disciple of Christ must not only keep the faith and live on it, but also profess it, confidently bear witness to it and spread it... Service of and witness to the faith are necessary for salvation. (*CCC*, 1816)

SCRIPTURE: *Jn* 15:16

Day 7: Be reborn

"I tell you the truth, unless you are born again, you cannot see the kingdom of God. (Jn 3:3)

We have been seeing this week how Jesus is the one the Old Testament and the Prophets are pointing to. The religious people at that time did not recognize him or understand his teaching!

"He came into the very world he created but the world didn't recognize him. He came to his own people, and even they rejected him. But to all who believed him and accepted him, he gave the right to become children of God. They are reborn – not with a physical birth resulting from human passion or plan, but a birth that comes from God " (*Jn* 1:10-13).

Jesus calls us who believe in him his children, and he wants us to see his kingdom now and to dwell with him in heaven for all eternity.

PRAYER: *Praise and thank you Lord for the joy of knowing that I am your child. By baptism and the filling of your Spirit, I am born again. Even though I do not see you I love you, and I praise you for the wonders of your kingdom I see around me and the hope I have of heaven!*

Catechism: Through Baptism we are freed from sin and reborn as sons of God; we become members of Christ, are incorporated into the Church and made sharers in her mission: "Baptism is the sacrament of regeneration through water in the word." (*CCC*, 1213)

Scripture: 1 *Jn* 3:1-2

~ A NEW COVENANT - A LAW OF LOVE ~
FIFTH WEEK

Day 1: Tell my people I love them

"But this is the new Covenant I will make with the people of Israel on that day", says the Lord. "I will put my instructions deep within them, and I will write them on their hearts. I will be their God and they will be my people. And they will not need to teach their neighbours saying, 'You should know the Lord.' For everyone, from the least to the greatest will know me already," says the Lord. "For I will forgive their wickedness and I will never again remember their sins." (Jr 31:33-34)

Today is that day! Our sins are forgiven and now God himself will cause us to love him through the power of his Holy Spirit. Everything that Jesus taught us in the Gospels is the truth, and only the Holy Spirit can lead us to live out this truth, (cf *Jn* 14:17), not out of fear but because he has put his love into our hearts (cf *Rm* 5:5).

PRAYER: *Lord fill me with your Spirit so that I can know how wide, how long, how high, and how deep your love is. You have done so much for me to know this love, my heart is full of praise and thanks to you.*

CATECHISM: 'God is love' and love is his first gift, containing all others. 'God's love has been poured into our hearts through the Holy Spirit who has been given to us.' (*CCC*, 733)

SCRIPTURE: *Ep* 3:18

Day 2: And what is love?

There is no greater love than to lay down one's life for one's friends. (*Jn* 15:13)

God's ways are not our ways, and when he talks of love he is talking about an extravagant, committed, sacrificial love: love that is willing to lay down its life for another. In the Eucharistic Prayer IV, the priest prays for the people: "That we might live no longer for ourselves but for him, who sent the Holy Spirit from you Father, as the first gift to those who believe, to complete his work on earth and bring us to the fullness of grace." Through the Holy Spirit we are called and empowered to live no longer for ourselves but to be like Jesus in his love.

PRAYER: *Mary wondered how it was possible that she could have a child. In the same way I find myself asking how can I be like You? Lord help me to believe as Mary did, that what you promise you will fulfil.*

CATECHISM: This love (the 'charity' of 1 *Co* 13) is the source of the new life in Christ, made possible because we have received 'power' from the Holy Spirit. (CCC, 735)

SCRIPTURE: *Lk* 1:45

Day 3: Sermon on the mount

Don't misunderstand why I have come. I did not come to abolish the Law of Moses or the writings of the prophets. No, I came to accomplish their purpose. (Mt 4:17)

In the Sermon on the Mount Jesus gave us the Law of love, and it seems so much harder than the law given on Mount Sinai! He said, "You have heard that it was said; you shall love your neighbour and hate your enemies...." (*Mt* 5:43). Jesus also tells us to turn the other cheek and not to get angry.

PRAYER: *Jesus, you said, "Keep on asking and you will receive what you ask for. Keep on seeking, and you will find. Keep on knocking, and the door will be opened to you..." (Lk 11:9-10) Thank you for this promise, I will ask, I will seek, and I will knock.*

CATECHISM: By this power of the Spirit, God's children can bear much fruit. He who has grafted us onto the true vine will make us bear 'the fruit of the Spirit:...love, joy, peace, patience, kindness, goodness, faithfulness, gentleness, self-control.' (*CCC*, 736)

SCRIPTURE: *Jn* 14:16-17

Day 4: Peter the rock

Jesus asked Simon Peter,"Simon, son of John, do you love me?" "Yes, Lord," Peter replied, "You know I love you." (*Jn* 21:15)

Peter had denied the Lord three times, and now after the Resurrection Jesus asks him, "Do you love me?" three times. The word that Jesus uses for love is '*Agapeo*', (Greek) referring to a sacrificial love. Peter answers twice with '*Philio*', meaning to love like a friend. Finally Jesus asks him, "Do you love me?" (*Philio*) and Peter feels upset. Jesus says, "Come follow me". When Jesus calls he gives us the grace to follow him. Years later, Peter was martyred for his love!

PRAYER: *Lord, you laid your life down for your sheep, and so often I am afraid to speak about you to those who do not know you. Forgive me for my lack of love, and fear of what others think, and fill me with your Spirit of boldness.*

CATECHISM: It is evident from its celebration that the effect of the sacrament of Confirmation is the full outpouring of the Holy Spirit as once granted to the apostles on the day of Pentecost... it gives us a special strength of the Holy Spirit to spread and defend the faith by word and action as true witnesses of Christ, to confess the name of Christ boldly, and never to be ashamed of the Cross. (*CCC*, 1302)

SCRIPTURE: *Ac* 4:13

Day 5: A new life

Therefore if anyone is in Christ, he is a new creation; the old has passed away, behold the new has come. All this is from God... (2 Co 5:17-18)

When we were baptized we received the life of the Spirit and this grace is the gift that God makes to us of his own life, filling us in order to bring healing and wholeness. Jesus through his Spirit lives in you and me. He grows within us through our daily intimacy with him. If you are anything like me I constantly know my own weakness, so it is important to hang onto the truth of God's word, that he is the treasure within our earthen vessels. By his grace, we can let go of our old ways and let him live his life in us.

PRAYER: *Love is patient and kind, not jealous, boastful or proud or rude. It does not demand its own way. It is not irritable, and it keeps no record of being wronged.... Lord have your way in me.*

CATECHISM: There is a need not only for instruction after Baptism, but also for the necessary flowering of baptismal grace in personal growth. (*CCC*, 1231)

SCRIPTURE: 2 *Co* 4:7

Day 6: Keep filling up

Don't be drunk with wine, but keep being filled with the Holy Spirit, singing psalms and hymns and spiritual songs among yourselves, and making music to the Lord in your hearts. (*Ep* 5:18-19)

Everyone knows that we need to check the petrol in the tank. It is impossible to run on empty! So it is with our lives in Christ. Each morning he wants to fill us with himself! How do we let him do that? Each person finds his own way for this daily infilling. Some may go to daily Mass or take an early morning walk to pray, or simply sit in a quiet corner. Most important is the faith that we have in his presence, and our receptiveness to his power to fill us.

PRAYER: *Jesus, fill me afresh today with your Holy Spirit, so I can overflow with love to all those around me, especially those closest and dearest to me. When I am weak you are strong!*

CATECHISM: As bodily nourishment restores lost strength, so the Eucharist strengthens our charity, which tends to be weakened in daily life; and this living charity wipes away venial sins. By giving himself to us, Christ revives our love and enables us to break our disordered attachments to creatures and root ourselves in him. (*CCC*, 1394)

SCRIPTURE: *Ga* 5:22-25

Day 7: Overflowing

If you only knew the gift God has for you and who you are speaking to, you would ask me, and I would give you living water. (Jn 4:10)

The above words were spoken to the Samaritan woman at the well. It was unheard of in those days that a Jew would talk to a Samaritan but Jesus' message is for all mankind. He saw her need and he gave, saying, "Anyone who drinks this water will soon become thirsty again. But those who drink the water I give will never be thirsty again. It becomes a fresh, bubbling spring within them, giving them eternal life."

PRAYER: *The Samaritan woman was so full of joy at meeting you, Lord, that immediately she ran back to her village saying, "Come and see a man who told me everything I ever did! Could he possibly be the Messiah?" Fill me with this same joy so that others may know you as their friend, Saviour and Lord.*

CATECHISM: The Holy Spirit is the living water 'welling up to eternal life' in the heart that prays. It is he who teaches us to accept it at its source: Christ. (*CCC*, 2652)

SCRIPTURE: 1 *P* 1:8-9

∾ THE KINGDOM OF GOD ∾
IS FOR ALL PEOPLE
SIXTH WEEK

Day 1: Heaven is touching earth

Go therefore, and make disciples of all the nations.
(Mk 16:15)

God's whole plan of Salvation was to woo his people back to himself with cords of love. He knew even before time began, that this love would mean sending his Son to die on the cross as the only way back to the Father. To all those who accepted his Son he gave the Holy Spirit, confirming that we are his child`ren, and the grace to live as Jesus did on earth. You and I who believe and know Jesus - the Church - are called to pray for and tell others this good news.

PRAYER: *So often Lord I am focused on my own problems, sins and needs. I get bogged down and lose the joy of my salvation. Forgive me, cleanse me and renew me with your Spirit, so that I can teach others to return to you. (cf Ps 51:12-13)*

CATECHISM: [Confirmation] perfects the common priesthood of the faithful, received in Baptism, and 'the

confirmed person receives the power to profess faith in
Christ publicly and as it were officially (*quasi ex officio*).'
(*CCC*, 1305)

SCRIPTURE: *Ps* 51:10-13

Day 2: Power and help from heaven

You will receive power when the Holy Spirit comes upon you, and you will be my witnesses, telling people about me everywhere - in Jerusalem, throughout Judea, in Samaria, and to the ends of the earth. (Ac 1:8)

1 Corinthians 12 describes gifts that the Holy Spirit gives to members of the Church for the building up of the body of Christ. Words of wisdom, knowledge, faith, healing, miracles, prophesy, discernment, tongues, and interpretation of tongues. It was these very gifts that the disciples received at Pentecost. They were told to wait in the city until they were clothed with power from on high. It is a renewal of this power that we need in our Church again.

PRAYER: *Lord, as the Church approaches Pentecost, help us to be open vessels to your Spirit. Fill us anew with your gifts so that we can become a channel to others.*

CATECHISM: [Grace] includes the gifts that the Spirit grants us to associate us with his work...There are furthermore *special graces*, also called *charisms*... Whatever their character – sometimes it is extraordinary, such as the gift of miracles or of tongues – charisms are oriented toward sanctifying grace, and are intended for the common good of the Church. (*CCC*, 2003)

SCRIPTURE: *Is* 61:1

Day 3: A praying Church

They all met together and were constantly united in prayer, along with Mary the mother of Jesus, and several other women and the brothers of Jesus. (Ac 1:14)

We must not undervalue the power of prayer. Behind every powerful evangelist are usually many people interceding. A trumpet is sounding today for intercessors to be united in prayer and purpose. We need to pray that the Church would be renewed as a shining light in the darkness. God has been using situations in your own life, to teach you to stand in your difficulties without despair. The Holy Spirit has been training you for a bigger battle which we are now going to enter through prayer for our Church.

PRAYER: *Father, thank you that as I pray for your Church, our prayers arise to you like incense with those of your Son who is continually making intercession for us at your right hand.*

CATECHISM: Mary 'aided the beginnings of the Church by her prayers.' In her association with the apostles and several women, 'we also see Mary by her prayers imploring the gift of the Spirit, who had already overshadowed her in the Annunciation.' (*CCC*, 965)

SCRIPTURE: *Ph 4:6-7*

Day 4: Exciting times

I don't have any silver or gold for you. But I'll give you what I do have. In the name of Jesus Christ the Nazarene, get up and walk! (Ac 3:6)

Peter and John were experiencing a new trust in the power of God. I wonder if they had had enough money, would they have known to walk in this new authority? Our own limitations are just what God uses to get us to pray in new ways. Jesus only did what he saw his Father doing. As we walk closely to Jesus he wants to give us revelation of his will, so that we can step out and pray for miracles. Unbelievers are searching for meaning and identity. God can only use our hands and hearts to bring his Kingdom to them.

Prayer: *Isaiah heard the Lord asking, "Whom should I send as a messenger to this people? Who will go for us? " I said, "Here I am, send me." Lord you are asking the same today. Please send your messengers into the harvest field today.*

Catechism: The ultimate purpose of mission is none other than to make men share in the communion between the Father and the Son in their Spirit of love. (*CCC*, 850)

Scripture: *Mt 9:37-38*

Day 5: Maranatha – come Lord Jesus

Blessed are the poor in Spirit for theirs is the Kingdom of God. (Mt 5:3)

Another translation says: "God blesses those who are poor and realize their need of him, for the Kingdom of Heaven is theirs." Not everyone will turn to the Lord and be saved. But it is our job to pray for everyone and to witness to everyone so at the right time, when the Lord comes again for his Bride, he will find us ready, washed clean in the blood of the Lamb. Let us pray for this day!

PRAYER: *Lord, you said that when you are lifted up you will draw all men to yourself. May your Church be renewed and lifted up by a new filling of your Holy Spirit this Pentecost so that all men may come to know you.*

CATECHISM: Because the Holy Spirit is the anointing of Christ, it is Christ who, as the head of the Body, pours out the Spirit among his members to nourish, heal and organize them in their mutual functions, to give them life, send them to bear witness, and associate them to his self-offering to the Father and to his intercession for the whole world. (*CCC*, 739)

SCRIPTURE: 1 *Tm* 3-5

The History of the Pentecost Novena

Blessed Elena Guerra

Elena Guerra, the Founder of the Sisters of the Holy Spirit, lived at the end of the 19th century in Italy. She

felt that is was important that the Catholic Church be renewed and return to the fervour of the first Christians at Pentecost. She called not only for the renewal of the Church, but also for Christian unity and a renewal of society, so that the face of the earth would be totally renewed. The key to this, she felt, was prayer and that the whole Church, like the first apostles, should return to the Upper Room to await a new Pentecostal outpouring.

Pope Leo XII

She wrote to the Pope, Leo XIII: "Pentecost is not over. In fact it is continuously going on in every time and in every place because the Holy Spirit desires to give Himself to all men and all who want Him can always receive Him, so we do not envy the apostles and the first believers; we only have to dispose ourselves like them to receive Him well, and He will come to us as He did to them."

As a result of her promptings the Pope issued several important documents about the Holy Spirit. He also asked the Church to celebrate a novena (nine days of prayer) every year between the Feasts of the Ascension and Pentecost to pray for the restoration and unity of the body of Christ.

At her request the Pope also invoked the Holy Spirit on the coming century by singing the *Veni Creator Spiritus* hymn on 1st January, 1901.

Vatican Council II

In the early 1960s Pope John XXIII, the newly elected pope, surprised everyone by calling the Vatican II Council to bring about the renewal of Church structures. He felt it was necessary to better equip the Church to meet the challenges of living and preaching the gospel to the world of the time. He prayed, "Renew Your wonders in this our day as by a new Pentecost."

John Paul II

One of the fruits of the Vatican II Council was a new openness to other Christians. On May 29th, 2004, Pope John Paul II, speaking at the First Vespers of Pentecost, again called for the 'spirituality of Pentecost 'to be spread in the Church 'as a renewed incentive to prayer, holiness, communion and proclamation.' He also gave his encouragement to the promotion of a Pentecost novena, under the title of the *'Burning Bush Initiative'*, which was being promoted by Kim Kollins, an American convert to Catholicism, who had been inspired in prayer, and by the writings of Blessed Elena, to promote this once again in the Church. She comments:

"We are in a time where God is calling his people to return anew to the Cenacle. It is a time to go beyond what is so often our normal scope of prayer – family, friends, or group or community, to pray with great fervour for the renewal of our hearts, of the Church, to pray for the unity of all Christians and the renewal of society and thereby 'a renewal of the face of the earth.' This call to adoration and intercession is both a right and a duty for all of us."

Benedict XVI

Since the beginning of his pontificate, Pope Benedict XVI has constantly spoken of the importance of prayer and the power of the Holy Spirit if the Church is to be effective. He has written:

"Are we going to discover the secret of the first Pentecost in the Church? Are we going to offer ourselves humbly to the renewing power of the Holy Spirit so that He can free us from our poverty and our total inability to carry out the task of proclaiming Jesus Christ to our fellow men? .... The Upper Room is the place where Christians allow themselves – in welcoming the Holy Spirit – to be transformed by prayer. But it is also the place from which one goes out to bring the fire of Pentecost to one's brothers."

Praying the Novena

Prayerful Preparation for a new Pentecost

After the journey of 40 days to this point, you are now invited to pray a Novena (nine days of prayer) which ends on the vigil of Pentecost.

Each day of the Novena is set out in the following pages. There is a special intercession for each day, accompanied by a passage of Scripture, a reflection, and a prayer. There are also additional prayers you can chose from if you wish.

What is important is to keep this attitude of prayer and intercession in your heart through each of these nine days, interceding for the church and the world – and that the Holy Spirit can renew both with his powerful love.

Day 1: Intercession - for Israel, the people of the Covenant

SCRIPTURE: *Is it possible that God abandoned his people? Out of the question. God never abandoned his own people to whom years ago he gave recognition ...on the contrary their failure has brought salvation to the Gentiles, in order to stir them to envy. (Rm 11)*

REFLECTION: God revealed himself to the Jewish people in a special way in history and prepared them to receive the Messiah. Jesus Christ, who was a Jew, was the fulfillment of all the Old Testament prophecies. When he came, his people rejected him because he was not the kind of Messiah they were expecting. But this was all part of God's plan, because the message of God's love and salvation is for the whole world not just the Jewish people. One of the signs that the Second Coming is drawing near, is that the Jews will recognize that Jesus is the Messiah.

PRAYER: *Father we thank you for the Jewish people. We thank you for their devotion and fidelity to you over the centuries. We repent of any sins of anti-Semitism on our part. We ask for your blessing upon them. Send them your Holy Spirit.*

Day 2: Intercession - for the renewal of the Church

SCRIPTURE: *And now I am sending upon you what the Father has promised. Stay in the city then, until you are clothed with power from on high. (Lk 24:49)*

REFLECTION: The Christian Church is the body of Christ on the earth. It is both human and divine. We are called to show the love and power of Christ to our world. Often our witness is marred, however, by our sins as individuals and as a body and this stops people seeing Jesus or listening to our message.

PRAYER: *Lord, we thank you for your Church on earth, the abiding expression of your love and reminder of your presence among us. We are sorry for the times we have let you down Lord, as a Church and as individuals. You know how weak we are. We pray that we as a body would reflect your face, your priorities and your values. We pray for all Church leaders, especially the Pope; grant them the wisdom and holiness they need to lead your people at this time in our history. Please send us your Holy Spirit, O Lord, and renew us. Fill us with your love and power and zeal for the Gospel. May our Church become alive with the Spirit of Pentecost once again.*

Day 3: Intercession - for the
unity of Christians

SCRIPTURE: *May they all be one, just as, Father, you are in me, and I am in you, so that they also may be one in us, so that the world may believe it was you who sent me. (Jn 17:21)*

REFLECTION: Right from the beginning the Christian body has been marred by divisions. There were arguments and jealousies among the apostles and in the early Christian community between Gentile Christians and Jewish believers. This has continued to this day. There are not only divisions between the different denominations and churches but within our own parishes, communities and fellowships. Our divisions and lack of love for each other, however, ruin our common witness as followers of Christ and are confusing to others outside the Church.

PRAYER: *Father, we thank you for all Christians, whatever their beliefs, for their love and devotion to you. Help us to love and respect each other, and to think the best of each other. Help us to support each other when we can and not to judge the different ways we might do things, knowing that you, Jesus, are at the heart of everything. Purify us, Lord, and help us to keep you at the centre, as the closer we are to you, the closer we will be to each other.*

Day 4: Intercession - for the renewal of society

SCRIPTURE: *Look, here God lives among human beings....*
He will wipe away all tears from their eyes. There will be
no more death, and no more mourning or sadness or
pain. The world of the past has gone. Then the One sitting
on the throne spoke: "Look, I am making the whole of
creation new." (Rv 21:3-5)

REFLECTION: Jesus came to bring about the kingdom of
God on earth – a world of love and peace and joy. He
showed us the way to do this, by turning away from
selfishness, giving our lives to him and drawing on his
power as the Son of God. The temptation of humankind,
however, is always to reject God and his authority and to
try and build utopia in our own strength - to create a
world where we are in charge. When we do this, however,
everything always crumbles into nothing.

PRAYER: *Father, we lift up to you our world and our*
society with all its brokenness and problems. We lift up to
you our governments and leaders. Guide them by your
Holy Spirit to make good decisions for the benefit of all.
In our own lives we suffer and inflict suffering on others
because of our sinfulness. Transform us in the power of
your Holy Spirit so that we may be agents of building a
civilization of love and of your kingdom.

Day 5: Intercession - for
conversion and holiness

SCRIPTURE: *Anyone who does not take up his cross and follow in my footsteps is not worthy of me. Anyone who finds his life will lose it, anyone who loses his life for my sake will find it.* (Mt 10:37-39)

REFLECTION: There is a danger of thinking holiness means human perfection, which we know from our own lives is impossible as we constantly fall. Holiness, however, means being set apart for God. Conversion is that primary decision we make in our life when we decide to live for God instead of ourselves. From then onwards God will use all the events of our life, if we let him, to help us to become more and more dependent on him and his Holy Spirit, and less and less on ourselves and our own strength. This is holiness – the growing presence of the Spirit of God within us directing our every thought and action, which will show itself in growing virtue and love of others.

PRAYER: *O Lord, so often we try and deal with life using our own limited vision and gifts. Help us to see people and events through your eyes. Fill us with your love. May we die to our egos and desires and grow in our knowledge and dependence on you. May all men and women be given the grace of conversion to know, love and follow you.*

Day 6: Intercession - for
reconciliation and healing

SCRIPTURE: *How delightful it is to live as brothers, all together!* (*Ps* 133:1)

REFLECTION: God has revealed to us that he is our Father and he calls us to love everyone as brothers and sisters. So often we find this so hard, particularly with those who hurt us the most - often those nearest to us - our families, work colleagues and fellow Christians. We hurt each other, justifying ourselves, condemning the other, in an endless cycle of pain and recrimination which slowly but surely destroy us. Jesus tells us the only way out of this destructive cycle is to forgive. Because of what Jesus has done on the Cross, we can draw on the strength of his Holy Spirit to do the things we cannot do on our own, particularly forgive our enemies, not just as individuals but as peoples and nations.

PRAYER: *O Jesus, you know all the people who have hurt me in my life. You know how hard I find it to forgive them. I lift up to you the wounds that exist, not just in my life but in the lives of my friends, family and my country. Nothing is impossible for you. May your reconciliation and peace and healing come to us all.*

Day 7: Intercession - for empowerment for evangelisation

SCRIPTURE: *And now I am sending upon you what the Father has promised. Stay in the city until you are clothed with the power from on high.* (*Lk* 24.49)

REFLECTION: The apostles spent three years with Jesus. They saw his miracles, experienced his love and heard his teaching. They loved him, yet in his moment of trial they ran away. They were not ready for the task to which Jesus was calling them. They still needed the empowerment of the Holy Spirit. We are the same today. If we are to share the Gospel message with others we too need the empowerment of the Holy Spirit. The only way that the Holy Spirit becomes truly effective in our lives is if we make a personal decision to repent of our sins and self-sufficiency and ask God to take control over our lives.

PRAYER: *Father, I acknowledge my sinfulness and pride. I repent of all self-sufficiency and I want to rely on you alone. Send down your Holy Spirit on me with all the charisms and gifts I need to be the effective Christian you want me to be. I lift up to you my prayer group, my parish community, my church. Send us your Spirit of love and power so that we may be instruments of the Kingdom of God.*

Day 8: Intercession - for the victory of the Holy Cross

SCRIPTURE: *May the God of our Lord Jesus Christ, the Father of glory, give you a spirit of wisdom and perception of what is revealed, to bring you to full knowledge of him. May he enlighten the eyes of your mind so that you can see what hope his call holds for you, how rich is the glory of the heritage he offers among his holy people, and how extraordinarily great is the power that he has exercised for us believers.* (Ep 1:17-20)

REFLECTION: Jesus could have come in strength and overcome evil by his Almighty power but he chose a different way. He seemingly allowed himself to be overcome by evil and died on a cross. But through the power of the Holy Spirit he rose again and demonstrated for all time the power of love to overcome evil. This truth has been shown again and again down through the ages.

PRAYER: *O Lord, help me to recognize those moments of death and resurrection in my own life. Those times when you are calling me to lay aside my strength and my power and to die to my own opinions for the good of unity, so that your will be done. May I never become depressed by the evil I see around me, but know that you are able to use all things for your purposes. Give me faith in the power of your love, that through your cross your kingdom will come on the earth.*

Day 9: Intercession - for a new outpouring of the Holy Spirit and His Gifts

SCRIPTURE: *Do not leave Jerusalem, but wait there for what the Father has promised. It is, he said, what you have heard me speak about. John baptized with water but not many days from now you are going to be baptized with the Holy Spirit. (Ac 1:4-5)*

REFLECTION: For the Church to do its job and be an effective agent for the Kingdom of God, it needs a continual empowerment of the Holy Spirit with all its charisms and gifts. Throughout history there have been outpourings of the Holy Spirit and this novena is to ask for another outpouring today to equip all God's people so that we can implement God's work of salvation on earth.

PRAYER: *Lord, I humbly pray that you would send your Holy Spirit down on me in the same way you did on the apostles in the Upper Room at Pentecost. Jesus, I give my life to you. Give me the grace to turn away from anything in my life that is an obstacle in my relationship with you. Help me to put you first in my life. Amen.*

Reflect upon the following words of Pope Benedict XVI on the Solemnity of Pentecost, (May, 2008):

"We read in the Acts of the Apostles that the disciples were praying all together in the Upper Room when the Holy Spirit descended upon them powerfully, as wind and fire. They then began to proclaim in many tongues the Good News of Christ's Resurrection (cf. 2:1-4).

This was the 'Baptism of the Holy Spirit' which had been foretold by John the Baptist: 'I baptize you with water,' he said to the crowds, 'but he who is coming after me is mightier than I... he will baptize you with the Holy Spirit and with fire' (*Mt* 3:11).

In fact, Jesus' entire mission aimed at giving the Spirit of God to men and women and baptizing them in his regenerative 'bath'. This was brought about with his glorification (cf. *Jn* 7:39), that is, through his death and Resurrection: then the Spirit of God was poured out in super-abundance, like a cascade capable of purifying every heart, extinguishing the fire of evil and kindling the flame of divine love in the world... Pentecost [is] the fulfillment of this promise and hence the culmination of Jesus' entire mission."

◦⌒ Novena Prayers to the Holy Spirit ⌒◦

Secret of Happiness

I am going to reveal to you the secret of sanctity and happiness. Every day for 5 minutes control your imagination and close your ears to all the noises of the world in order to speak to that Divine Spirit, saying to Him:

O Holy Spirit, beloved of my soul, I adore you. Enlighten me, Guide me, Strengthen and Console me. Tell me what I should do. Give me your orders. I promise to submit myself to all that you desire of me and to accept all that you permit to happen to me. Let me only know your will.

If you do this your life will flow along happily and serenely and full of consolation, even in the midst of trials. Grace will be proportionate to the trial and you will arrive at the grace of merit. This submission to the Holy Spirit is the secret to sanctity.

(*Cardinal Mercier's Prayer*)

Renew your wonders in this our day as by a new Pentecost.

(*Pope John XXIII*)

Father, pour out your Spirit upon your people, and grant us a new vision of your glory, a new experience of your power, a new faithfulness to your service, that your love may grow among us and your Kingdom come: through Christ Our Lord. Amen.

God the Holy Spirit, Comforter and Sanctifier, melt our hearts that we may accept your love. Renew our minds that we may know your truth. Strengthen our wills that we may serve you faithfully. Through Christ Our Lord. Amen.

May He grant you to be strengthened with might through His Spirit in the inner self. (*Ep* 3.16)

❧ DAILY PRAYERS TO THE HOLY SPIRIT ❧

In the morning

Relax your body…
Calm your mind and your imagination…
Affirm that God is present…
Ponder these words from Scripture..
Be filled with the Spirit
Be guided by the Spirit
Walk by the Spirit

Prayer for guidance

Father in heaven: Yours is a Spirit of truth and love. Pour that same Holy Spirit into my body, my mind, my soul. Preserve me this day from all illusions and false inspirations and reveal your presence and purposes to me in a way that I can understand.

I thank you that you will do this, while giving me the ability to respond through Jesus Christ Our Lord. Amen.

Pause for a moment's reflection.

At night

Relax your body…
Calm your mind and your imagination…
Affirm that God is present…
Consider these words…

"God's presence is not discerned at the time when it is upon us, but afterwards when we look back upon what is gone and over."

(Cardinal Newman)

Use one or more of the following prayers:

Prayers for discernment

Father in heaven, help me to recall with gratitude those occasions when I was aware of your presence today and to savour again, what you meant to me.

Pause for a moment's reflection.

Help me to become aware of the promptings and inspirations you have given me today and to know whether I responded to them or not.

Pause for a moment's reflection.

Enlighten my heart to recognize any unloving mood, attitude, desire or action that saddened your Holy Spirit today.

Pause for a moment's reflection.

Final prayer

Father in heaven, thank you for the gift of your Spirit. Today, it has urged me to see you more clearly, to love you more dearly, and to follow you more nearly. As for my shortcomings, please forgive them. And now, bless me as I sleep, so that refreshed by your Spirit, I may rise to praise you, through Jesus Christ our Lord. Amen.[1]

Veni Creator Spiritus

Come Holy Ghost, Creator come
From thy bright heavenly throne,
Come take possession of our souls,
And make them all thine own.

Thou who are called the Paraclete,
Best gift of God above,
The living spring, the living fire
Sweet unction and true love.

Thou who are sevenfold in thy grace,
Finger of God's right hand;
His promise, teaching little ones
To speak and understand.

---

[1] Permissu Ordinarii Dioc.Dublinen.

O guide our minds with thy blest light,
With love our hearts inflame;
And with thy strength, which ne'er decays,
Confirm our mortal frame.

Far from us drive our deadly foe;
True peace unto us bring
And through all perils lead us safe
Beneath thy sacred wing.

Through thee may we the Father know,
Through thee the eternal Son,
And thee the Spirit of them both,
Thrice blessed Three in One.

All glory to the Father be,
With his co-equal Son;
The same to thee, great Paraclete,
While endless ages run.

(Ascribed to Rabanus Maurus (776-856) translated from the Latin.)

Novena to the Holy Spirit

Before he ascended into heaven, Jesus instructed his apostles to remain in Jerusalem for Pentecost, and to pray for the Holy Spirit. These 'nine days' have given rise to the Christian 'novena' or nine days of fervent prayer, in preparation for important feasts or for special needs or intentions. With St Philip Neri as his guide, Fr Bochanski leads us through nine days of prayer, each linked to a fruit of the Holy Spirit: love, joy, peace, patience, kindness, goodness, faithfulness, gentleness, and self-control. With down-to-earth reflections from St Philip and Cardinal Newman included, this booklet can be used at any time throughout the year.

ISBN: 978 1 86082 381 7

CTS Code: D 678

Road to Pentecost

This booklet was originally commissioned and published by the English National Service Committee (NSC) for Catholic Charismatic Renewal to help promote the culture of Pentecost in the Church called for by Pope Benedict XVI. This edition of the booklet is a revised edition jointly published with the Catholic Truth Society.

A simple CTS leaflet of Pentecost Novena prayers and readings is also available for parishes in packs of 25.

The NSC support Catholic Evangelisation Services (CES) which produces the popular CaFÉ DVD resources for parishes *www.faithcafe.org*

The NSC is also responsible for Goodnews, a bi-monthly magazine which seeks to encourage Catholics in their faith and to grow in their understanding of the charisms of the Holy Spirit. It also features inspiring stories of personal conversion, transformed lives and healings. The annual subscription is £13.95 a year (25 euros Ireland) – cheques payable to CREW Trust. Write to Goodnews, Allen Hall, 28 Beaufort Street, London SW3 5AA Tel: 020 7352 5298

For further information about the Catholic Charismatic Renewal you can log on to their website ccr.org.uk